WHEN FELLOWSHIP REALLY COUNTS

Taking it to the Next Level

By

Judy A. Wyndham

Copyright © 2015 by Judy A.Wyndham

When Fellowship Really Counts
Taking it to the Next Level

by Judy A.Wyndham

Printed in the United States of America

ISBN 9781498425513

All rights reserved solely by the author. The author guarantees all contents are original and do not infringe upon the legal rights of any other person or work. No part of this book may be reproduced in any form without the permission of the author. The views expressed in this book are not necessarily those of the publisher.

Scripture quotations taken from the King James Version (KJV) – public domain

www.xulonpress.com

Table of Contents

Foreword vii
Dedication ix
Endorsements for When Fellowship Really Counts xi
Introduction: Chapter 1 Do You Have a Desire to be
                Around Other Christians? 13
Chapter 2 Outdo One Another in Love 17
Chapter 3 Fellowship With God is Special 19
Chapter 4 Fellowship is Important..23
Chapter 5 Basis of Our Unity..25
Chapter 6 Refreshing the Saints in Fellowship.............................27
Chapter 7 Are you Dating or in Fellowship? 29
Chapter 8 Passing the Mantle of Fellowship to the
          Next Generation 31
Chapter 9 Fellowship amid Military Personnel 33

Conclusion 37
References 39
Biography 41
About the Author...
Endorsement by: Bishop Jesse & Darlene Wilson, Gladys
              Kneeland, Chaplain Anthony J. Cook,
            and Mary Hallom

Foreword

Philippians 1:4-5 resounds in my heart as the Apostle Paul offers thanksgiving and praise to God saying, "Always in every prayer of mine for you all making request with joy, for your fellowship in the gospel from the first day until now." What Paul was saying here is that the mutual faith in the gospel and working with him to share the good news creates a relationship or partnership of trust and devotion. When you love being with someone, you get involved with what they are doing. That's fellowship.

Judy Wyndham

Dedication

This book is dedicated to my Lord and Savior Jesus Christ and the Holy Spirit who comforts me, keeps me, and called me to write this book for the people of God and the cause of Christ. To my mother of ninety-four years young, Mrs. Evelena Clark, who had the vision of education for her family when she was unable to attend college after graduating from high school. Her values of coming together, supporting the family, prayer, and fellowship have resounded in my heart forever and I am honored to submit to her godly upbringing and faith that has moved mountains in my life. Truly, it was the faith of my grandmother Almeta, grandmother Pearl, and mother Evelena through the Holy Spirit that inspires me to write this book. I also want to honor my pastor, Chaplain Anthony J. Cook whose godly dedication to fellowship on a regular basis and being around the saints helped keep him while his spouse served in deployment this year.

Chaplain Cook creates opportunities for fellowship when it is farthest from the minds of others and it works. His leadership style through fellowshipping after having preached the engrafted word is unique; it accomplishes its purpose and reaches the hearts of those it is intended to touch.

I am further dedicating this book to a special Senior Pastor, Bishop Jesse T. and Elect Lady Darlene Wilson of Center of Deliverance COGIC, who enjoys fellowship on every level and have gone above and beyond the call of duty to ensure their fellowship is maintained whenever and wherever we assemble together.

It was Bishop Thomas Weeks III who instilled in me there is a writer in you. He encouraged us to write books and create businesses. His best seller, *Millionaires, Don't Go to Sleep Without Brushing Their Teeth: How to Awaken the Millionaire Within*, set the stage for me to go higher in the realm of the spirit and take a closer look at how God was going to make this happen in my life.

Last but not least, to my five year old granddaughter Chloe Nicole Gore who at my request got on her knees with me, laid hands on my head, and prayed for my mind to be filled with God's thoughts and God's spirit would take control of my mind so I could write this book. I can truly say after seven hours of writing, it is finished. Glory to God!

Judy Wyndham

Endorsements for
When Fellowship Really Counts

Fellowship is important in a world that is deeply distressed, troubled, and full of broken relationships. Judy Wyndham has given us a refreshing and restoring perspective of the importance of biblical fellowship. To those who long for true fellowship, may you be enriched by reading this book.

My wife and I encourage you to meditate on the pages of this book and explore the five ways to refresh your fellowship with God and take your relationship with the body of Christ to another level.

Bishop Jesse and Darlene Wilson
Prelate and First Lady
Hawaii Jurisdiction COGIC Inc.

Minister Judy Wyndham is a great friend, mother, grandmother, and anointed Woman of God! I have known Minister Judy for approximately twenty years. Over the course of those years, I have seen how God has truly blessed her and her family. He has answered prayers and opened doors for her that only God could do! Minister Judy brings out how important it is to fellowship with like-minded Saints and backs her statements up with scriptures. She reminds us that fellowship should always be a part of our lives where we invite the Lord to be a part of what we are doing. She does not neglect to remind us to love the unlovable. She also focuses on words of wisdom gleaned from her pastor Chaplain Anthony J. Cook.

I consider myself truly blessed to be a sister in Christ to Minister Judy; it is my privilege and an honor to endorse her book. I believe reading this book and meditating on the referenced scriptures will be life changing regarding our fellowship with one another.

Mother Gladys Kneeland
Mother's Board of Christian Faith Fellowship Church
Zion, IL

Fellowship has created and enhanced a number of meaningful relationships. If a person neglects to engage in fellowship, that person fails to engage in a vital source needed for spiritual and emotional resilience. In other words, they hinder their ability to recover quickly from, illness, depression, and adversity. As a pastor, I have witnessed firsthand the power of fellowship. When people initially come to the church spiritually and emotionally depleted, after experiencing the loving authentic fellowship of the church members, their spiritual and emotional states are renewed and regenerated. Judy Wyndham's new book on fellowship is timely and relevant opening a new perspective on the subject of fellowship. I hope that you take the opportunity to read this great book and apply its principles.

Maj. Chaplain Anthony J. Cook (U.S. Army Chaplain)

God has placed on her heart the will to be obedient to the spirit and to embark on this journey we can all identify with as fellowship. This reading will explain the importance of love, forgiveness, and fellowship amongst believers in Christ from all walks of life. I am so very proud of you, Ms. Judy Wyndham. May God Bless you on this book and all future endeavors.

Love Always,
Gospel and Inspirational Radio Personality
and Granddaughter MaryAnna Hallom
www.soarradio.com

Introduction

CHAPTER 1

Do You Have a Desire to be Around Other Christians?

I believe in this day, age, and dispensation of grace, fellowship — whether with the saints of God, family, or friends — is often neglected especially in the life of a Christian. No one can make it in this world alone; we need each other. What is fellowship? Fellowship is that important part of our faith where we come together to support one another in an experience that allows us to learn, gain strength, and show the world exactly who God is. We each have a purpose to demonstrate God on this earth and show aspects of His love to those around us (Mahoney, 2014). The key to unity and growth is doing life together, drawing new people, and deepening relationships (Josh Hunt, 2014; Discover LifetreeCafe.com).

Growing up in the church, this word "fellowship" was associated more with the potluck meal that carried on after church or meeting together with other church members for some much-needed time together to share our love for one another. Matthew 18:20 says, "Where two or three are gathered together in my name, there I am in the midst of them." Fellowship should always be a part of our lives where we invite the Lord to be a part of what we are doing. If what we are doing cannot invite Him in, then we shouldn't do it. 1 John 3:16 says "we ought to lay down our lives for the brothers." When we lay down our lives, we are setting aside quality time to engage in conversation and to pour into the lives of others who need that close contact with us at the moment.

We are saying, "you matter the most to me now and this is where I want to be: involved in your life. How it is developing matters to me." Chaplain Anthony Cook says, "Fellowship is important." It is vital to the life of the church and everyone in the church that desires spiritual growth. The fellowship after a retirement speech was most important to Chaplain Cook because this is where he can share the love of God and meet and greet people who he may not have had the opportunity otherwise. This is an important highlight of his day because it strengthens his resolve in doing the work of the ministry. Just being he to others is what he does best. People enjoy his warmth and humility along with the humor.

Most people need fellowship, but are afraid to ask for it. A lot of times we desire the fellowship, but are afraid we will be rejected by those we focus on for that intimate time. I like it when someone else, such as the pastor, requests that intimacy ("into me you see") where you get to see the real me and learn something about me you didn't know before. We have not because we ask not (James 4:2). If we were to ask for the fellowship with those we desire to be with, it would happen, and they are probably waiting to fulfill your desire to fellowship with them. For a moment, I thought I was one of those who was afraid to ask, but after thinking it over, I am not actually afraid to ask, but don't ask and am well aware that I should.

Perhaps you don't have the resources required for your part in the fellowship and it's keeping you from fellowshipping with those around you who need your love or you are an introvert who keeps to yourself and doesn't want to be around people. Jesus our Lord can fix all that. Psalm 55:14 reminds us of how: "We used to take sweet counsel together; within God's house we walked in company." When you have walked with others in the congregation or in life, it should be easy to find time to be with them. Some people have been through the thick and the thin together—all kinds of heartache and pain, emotional ups and downs—and need to encourage one another.

According to Chaplain Cook, so many others are afraid to ask and that is his reason for creating opportunities for people to fellowship together. He is a "people person" and enjoys seeing others happy. The success of it is when they all come together with something to share—whether it's a dish, conversation or servant's heart—the message and mission is still the same.

I think that's funny because people always want to fellowship with me, but I don't always desire to because I want to be alone just to think. I have to remember to come out of my comfort zone because there is a time for everything under the sun. There is a time to fellowship and a time not to fellowship. We have to be able to discern those times and submit to God's will for them. I am like the singer Al Green, sometimes tired of being alone, but craving fellowship, and there are those times I long for quiet and peace. Sometimes I rush back home just to get in a quiet place and there are times I desire to glean from others what God is saying.

Why is it that public people thrive on their private time and seek out private places where they are unnoticed by the public? Some people ought not to be alone and should always seek out the fellowship with other believers to strengthen their inner being, especially when the world, the flesh, and the devil is weighing them down and oppressing them. That private time with God helps sharpen your wit and wisdom for the fellowship to come and depending on how much you will pour out, as you engage with others, it will come out decently and in order. You will be more alert. You have to be willing and available to fellowship with other Christians and people in general: coworkers, family, and friends are all a part of the circle of fellowship. How we avail ourselves opens the doors for all sorts of great and endless possibilities.

Chapter 2

Outdo One Another in Love

Romans 12:10 says, "Love one another with brotherly affection. Outdo one another in showing honor or preferring one another." For instance, you took me to a great restaurant last week for fellowship, so next time I am taking you beyond that. Outdoing one another is saying, "I want to give you my best and most blessed because you showed me your best love."

My best love could also be that I suggest you for that job position rather than myself because of your love and humility. I humble myself to say, "You are the best for that job," especially when I know you are. I believe this is when we can enjoy our greatest fellowship—when we humble ourselves and take a more lowly opinion of ourselves to exalt someone else.

At the time of writing this, it is Pastor's Appreciation Month and some will try to outdo others at blessing their pastor. The pastor is not aware this is transpiring, but will be the recipient of a lavished love like he has never known before from the congregation. When you love someone, you want to be near them and involved in what they are involved in. I want to covenant with you to agree with you, think like you do, and see things the way you see do.

We can outdo one another in this because we want nothing but the best and we have to be willing to go all out to see that their happiness is first and we in turn receive our joy and satisfaction from seeing them fulfilled. Jesus Christ was the fulfillment of the law and the prophets. He knew the people could not keep all of the law, which was a requirement, so He came to fulfill it all with an act of divine love.

This kind of love is not a slippery term whereby we manipulate another into some mere passion or satisfaction, but a sincere love without motives and is practical, ordinary and blunt. It is the meat and potatoes we should be serving up daily as disciples of Christ while we display real devotion, honor one another, share with one another when in need, welcome others into our home, rejoice when others rejoice, weep when they weep, and last but not least, live in harmony and bring vitality to the body of Christ on earth. The most important thing you can do for another human being is to love them. This is how we promote unity in the body of Christ by our love to one another (Richards, 1990).

Chapter 3

Fellowship with God Is Special

1 John 1:3 tells us, "that which we have seen and heard we proclaim also to you, so that you too may have fellowship with us; and indeed our fellowship is with the Father and with His son Jesus Christ." If we confess with our mouth the Lord Jesus Christ and believe in our hearts God hath raised him from the dead we shall be saved (Romans 10:9). That heart fellowship must be established with God first, then with one another. One thing about the Father and His Son Jesus Christ is that they are everywhere and always present with us. They wrap themselves around us with a garment of light when we are walking in love.

God has pledged us for the purpose of His presence and we have been called to carry the tabernacle saturated and elevated through the anointing into every place where the soles of our feet shall tread. We are separated and elected for the Glory of God. Even when we come to fellowship, we stay away from the rubbish because we need revelation and breakthrough (Evans, 2012). Fellowship is like wise men on a journey to receive and impart. God is using us in fellowship to send His gifts to those who need them and to put a seed in the right place. Since I have access by faith to the kingdom of God, I desire to work for God in that fellowship setting where others can sit near listening and learning. When we have fellowship with God, He draws near to be with us. Fellowshipping is a mission and God wants to be in the center.

Luke 24:13 says, "That very day two of them were going to a village named Emmaus, about seven miles from Jerusalem, and they were talking with each other about all these things that had happened. While they were talking and discussing together, Jesus himself drew near and went with them." Today we go to our destination for fellowship, perhaps your favorite restaurant or the beach or in the comfort of your own backyard. You gather together with friends to discuss things and talk about the goodness of the Lord or family life and society in general, God draws near to go with you and to be with you while you fellowship. Devoting yourself to the Apostle's teaching and the fellowship to the breaking of bread and prayers (Acts 2:42).

What a better way to spend the day than staying faithful to the one who called you and keeps in line with what you have been taught? Teaching others is true fellowship; all while you eat, drink and be merry. Stay alert in prayer to what is said from others so you will know what to pray for them. Fellowship encourages us and challenges us to stay accountable to one another, and all the more as we see the day approaching. We cannot neglect this part of the word, because it is obedience to Christ. We have come together in fellowship with God and each other to bear one another's burdens (Galatians 6:2) and to show hospitality to each other without complaining (1 Peter 4:9) (Evans, 2012).

Let us be sure that we are not using this freedom we have in Christ as a license to sin. In other words, do not be unequally yoked together in fellowship with unbelievers. What fellowship has light with darkness, or righteousness with lawlessness? I am not going to use going to the club to party as a means of fellowshipping, because that would be an excuse to sin. Paul told the church at Ephesus in Ephesians 5:5 not to have any fellowship with the unfruitful works of darkness or to no more be tossed about with every wind of doctrine (Ephesians 4:14-16). When we come together, scripture says we come with a song or a hymn and we take the opportunity to do good to everyone, especially everyone in the household of faith (Galatians 6:10). I am not going to go out and cast my pearls before swine, or give what is holy to the dogs. You get my gist.

I couldn't possibly stir you up to good works at the club while we talk trash, drink liquor, and dance the night away. Hebrews 10:24-25 admonishes us to consider how we stir one another up to good works, not neglecting to meet together, as is the habit of some, but encouraging one another, and all the more as we see the Day approaching. The day of the Lord is soon approaching and we had better be about the Father's business of encouraging one another when we come together to fellowship and stir one another up to good works, not in drunkenness or carousing, but doing good and not evil. A friend will and cannot say, "Never," because the welcome will never end (Evans, 2012).

Chapter 4

Fellowship Is Important

When we come together in fellowship, it is like a picture of God. We each in our own uniqueness display all the graces of God to the world. Since no one is perfect and we all have sinned and come short of the glory of God, our purpose outshines all the sin that tries to perpetrate. We are demonstrating God's goodness and glory when we come together. It's like taking a recipe for something truly delicious and adding all the necessary ingredients to make it delicious. They can only accomplish this purpose if they are blended together and nothing left apart. That's how it is in fellowship—we all display God's glory when we are together and on one accord.

Being in fellowship helps us to remember that God makes us strong no matter where we are in our faith. Other believers give us the opportunity to grow in our faith and when we believe, it becomes excellent food to our souls (Mahoney, 2014). We have to deal with a cold-hearted world that really doesn't care if you are Christian or not; they question our beliefs and persecute us for the sake of Christ. It's difficult to evangelize when people are so cold and indifferent, but when we spend time in fellowship with other believers we are strengthened for battle (Mahoney, 2014). Put on the whole armor of God so you can stand against the wiles of the devil (Ephesians 6:11).

We are all going to have some bad moments in life such as money problems, loss of a loved one, anger, or a crisis in faith, but when we are feeling low and disillusioned, we can go to the rock that is higher, the solid rock of Christ, and His word through a human vessel whose heart is right before Him is ready to help with the challenge. This is the time when fellowship is important as we keep our eyes on Jesus and He provides what we need in the darkest times through those who can encourage us and help with the process of healing and deliverance.

Since we are not alone in this world and there are other believers everywhere, He wanted us to come together so we would understand and know that we are not alone in this world or in what we go through. This thing called fellowship causes us to make lasting relationships that make us feel like we are at home and never by ourselves in this world (Mahoney, 2014). We are teaching each other so many things we knew nothing about.

1 Cor.12:21 (NLT) says, "The eye can never say to the hand, I don't need you. The head cannot say to the feet, I don't need you". Christian fellowship is definitely one of the signs of a true believer (1 John 1:7). Going to church and being around other believers doesn't make you a Christian, but if you are a true Christian, you will want to go to church and/or have a desire to be around other believers on a regular basis *(DeYoung, 2012)*.

CHAPTER 5

The Basis of Our Unity

Christ has brought us together because we all accept the same doctrine and teaching of the Bible and we let the word of God settle the matter. We don't do wrong for the friendship or fellowship or let pride dictate how we fellowship. We koinonia or have communion and fellowship as we share things in common or from the heart.

We partner together or take covenant in our sharing. We love and accept one another with all of our idiosyncrasies, faults, misunderstandings, and misgivings. All our failures are not considered in our basis for our unity because all have sinned and come short of the glory of God (Abrams III, 2014).

If we have a genuine concern and spirit of restoration in our fellowship one to another, then if anyone is overtaken in a fault we which are spiritual, we can restore such with a spirit of meekness (or what-can-I-do-for-you attitude), as we consider ourselves lest we also be tempted (Galatians 6:1-2). It is going to require much prayer to bear burdens of the spiritually and morally weak and fallen and fellowship with these persons praying them through their offenses.

We have to have a common concern where we lead them to repentance and confession. James 5:16 says to "confess your faults to one another and pray for one another, that ye may be healed and the effectual fervent prayer of a righteous man availeth much." In other words—be that person someone can confess his or her faults to so healing can take place. Make sure you are living holy and righteous so the prayers you offer for them can avail or reach heaven and do damage to the devil's kingdom (Abrams III, 2014).

CHAPTER 6

Refreshing the Saints in Fellowship

When Paul thought about Philemon, he thought about all the joy and comfort he brought to others and himself. Philemon 1:7 admonishes us with, "I have derived much joy and comfort from your love, my brother, because the hearts of the saints have been refreshed through you." We ought to want to be like Philemon: a joy and comfort to others in a dry and thirsty land (Psalm 63:1, John 7:38). Being in a place they can drink the water of life an oasis when they are parched and ready to faint is significant.

Jesus said in Matthew 10:42, "Whoever gives one of these little ones a cup of cold water because he is truly a disciple, truly, I say to you, he will in no means lose his reward." There is a reward attached to the ministry of refreshment and that is important to Jesus. There are five ways we can refresh the saints (Bloom, 2013).

1. By loving and trusting Jesus. Philemon 1:5: "When I hear of the love and faith that you have toward the Lord Jesus. Love the Lord all ye His saints for God is love." This kind of love gives us the resources to love our neighbor as ourselves. When we are drinking the living water then and only then can we quench someone else's thirst.
2. When we have love for the saints: Talk is cheap. We ought to love not only in word, but in deed too. Meeting their needs

with every resource that we have (1 John 3:17). We are responsible to refresh the needy saints in our faith community.
3. As we share our faith: The full knowledge to become effective of every good thing that is within us for the sake of the gospel (Philemon 1:6). There are some weary saints in our fellowship that need refreshment of our shared faith; like the fishes and the loaves, they need a liberal portion.
4. Set your family members free to serve the Kingdom: Philemon 1:13: We have to think of the kingdom needs now and not our household needs when dealing with the bondservant or family members who come to Christ. Release our family members for the sake of refreshing the saints.
5. Transform your home into an embassy: Prepare a guest room for me (Philemon 1:22).

Our homes are not our castles, but embassies as Christians or Ambassadors for Christ, God has given us to refresh the saints and help the unbelievers become fellow citizens with all the saints (Ephesians 2:19).

A place that refreshes is an oasis place. Brothers and sisters around us are battling it out in spiritual warfare with a futile world and they are in need of our encouragement (Romans 8:20) (Bloom, 2013). Righteousness exalts a nation, but sin is a reproach to any people. Fellowship ought to leave a deposit in each of us. Too many times, others draw from us and never deposit any encouragement or uplifting words. Doc McStuffins would probably diagnose you with fellowshipitis, which is too much fellowship with those who don't deposit something good.

Make sure your fellowship is with God first so you can fellowship with others. You can't have too much fellowship with God, but with man you can overdo it to the point of being weary.

CHAPTER 7

Are You Dating or in Fellowship?

*D*ating for a Christian is considered a form of fellowship. When kept in its proper context, it absolutely puts two people in a position to get to know each other better by spending quality time together in Godly fellowship. I believe people are tired of old, run-down relationships that lead nowhere, especially not to love and marriage. Dating—which should be shifted to godly fellowship—with others present is a better approach to spending time with an individual from a new perspective and God's point of view. As we begin to look for solutions to relationship problems from the past, we see where we should do something we have never done before in order to produce better results.

Perhaps if we wore provocative clothing or were flirtatious it wouldn't require that when we submit to God's way of fellowshipping. Psalm 119:9 (NASB) says, "How can a young man cleanse his way? By keeping it according to thy word." This word is for young women as well. If we do not wander from the commandments God has given us—especially that we love the Lord with all of our heart, soul, mind, and strength—we want to please Him in everything we do.

Sure, the spirit of lust, perversion, fornication, adultery, and every other evil thing will be there knocking at the door of our heart to see how we respond, but we have to stand strong against it with the word we have received and learned from God. This is so God can get into our lives the good things He purposed for us. Many times we settle for less than God's best because we are anxious. We should be anxious for nothing, but take the time to pray through the anxiety so it can leave and the peace of God can come and take the rule in your heart and not the anxiety.

A young lady or man can look around at all the failed relationships and see that if the old way worked, there would be more successful relationships. They can look at their own lives in most cases. If you want someone better than you've had in the past, start doing the things necessary to attract a better quality of person for your life. In most cases, you don't have to do anything but submit to God in His righteousness and the right ones will be given to you.

If you are underhanded, deceptive, cheating, and a liar, you will probably gravitate toward those of like mind. When we are on our fellowship date stage (if it gets that far), then we should be quick to hear and slow to speak. In other words—develop a gentle and quiet spirit. Wearing clothing that is beautiful, yet modest doesn't expose all your fleshly qualities or is provocative, but does reveal an inner quality of wisdom and good judgment.

Men are attracted to women who make wise choices and not loose ones. Men, women want men who have direction and purpose and can lead them in righteousness. I want a man who can take me to my next level in life and ministry. If he doesn't know where he is going, I can't follow him. I am praying for you that you will seek the Lord in relationships and not be afraid of His choices, so you can get who is just right for you. It's called God's perfect will. He will allow your will but you may not be pleased once you get it or the initial shock wears off. Remember: focusing on marriage is wrong, according to Matthew 6:33. Seek God and fellowship with Him according to Proverbs 18:22. A man is supposed to find a wife so wait for that right man to approach you, the one that is perfect for you. Let love be in the mix. Provide what is best for me. The secret of a confident woman is that her confidence is in God.

CHAPTER 8

Passing the Mantle of Fellowship to the Next Generation

*I*n Matthew 19:14, Jesus said, "Suffer the little children, and forbid them not, to come unto me: for of such is the kingdom of heaven." Our children enjoy fellowship with other children just as we adults do. They come together with other children and teens to enjoy their time of interaction and play. They love to play, talk, and hangout until they get tired. Children may have sleepovers, play video games, watch movies, and eventually go to sleep. It stimulates fun when children come together. They share thoughts, games, and a room for a day and also get to see what it's like inside another friend's home.

Sometimes they tell jokes just for the laughter and some on a more serious note. Children love to fellowship every chance they get, sometimes every month due to their busy schedules, but some have been cut short in order to complete homework. Psalm 78:4-5 says:

We will not hide them from our children, showing to the generation to come, the praises of the Lord, and His strength, and His wonderful works that He hath done. For he established a testimony in Jacob, and appointed a law in Israel, which he commanded our fathers, that they should make known to their children.

My grandson Malik says they do good stuff like ministering to the homeless, that's fellowship to him. Good fellowship for children and teens can be a great meal at their favorite restaurant—especially when someone else is footing the bill. Yes we should never forbid our children the privilege of fellowship with their peers when it is in their best interest to do so. Birthday parties are a fantastic form of fellowship and help children bond with new acquaintances. I asked a bunch of sixth graders what fellowship meant to them and the answer they gave was astounding because I never would have guessed playing cards on the rug as they so insistently do was the highlight of their fellowship and day together.

Going to the movies, shopping at the mall, tea parties, walking pets, traveling, sports, camping, spending time with others, being a fashion consultant to your mom while shopping and hanging out, were the most popular responses on what fellowship meant to them. I then asked what were some of the attitudes to avoid while fellowshipping and they responded with refrain from teasing, making mean statements, bullying, name-calling, lying, punching, talking trash, kidding, playing tricks, and being disobedient.

Some of the things you can do to counteract the negative behavior when fellowshipping is to be trustworthy, helpful, and friendly. Proverbs 18:24 says, "A man that hath friends must show himself friendly: there is a friend that sticks closer than a brother." Be kind, courteous, cheerful, brave, clean, and generous. You know often times people disagree because they don't understand one another. Misunderstandings prevent unity and bad suspicion, mistrust, and hostility. I believe these sixth graders got it right and we could learn from them. Fellowship should create a mutual atmosphere of love and respect, so let's do unto others as we would have them do unto us.

Chapter 9

Fellowship amid Military Personnel

It is important for those serving in the military—Christians in particular—to continue in godly fellowship and the breaking of bread with other believers. Even as they PCS from duty station to duty station, fellowship with the people of God helps strengthen the individual or family as they enter a new environment and as they seek a new body of believers for the next few years. God is building an army; His body and fellowship with other believers is the catalyst in this building process. Single military personnel can stay accountable by seeking godly, responsible fellowship where their values are not compromised and they are respected and held in high esteem for the integrity they endeavor to walk in. Even when deployed, the temptation to straddle the fence interferes with the mission ahead. The devil is walking about as a roaring lion seeking whom he may devourer.

If we let our guard down, he slips in to deceive us because we are not watching, discerning, or praying. Young men and women in deployment often use church as a scapegoat to get out of their obligation to really be in chapel or church by going in an alternate direction. My word of wisdom to military personnel is to frankly be accountable to one of your peers. Bad things can happen to good people and they do, especially when you're in the wrong place at the wrong time. Go to church or chapel and learn how to conduct yourself as a good soldier when in uniform and when out. There are guidelines to follow as a soldier when in the public eye and scrutiny of the Lord. While traveling, visiting the USOs for fellowship with other soldiers and volunteers can make a difference. When there is no expression, it can lead to depression. So meet and greet others show yourself friendly so you can win friends.

Fellowship is like two people on a ship going in the same direction. Remember God is always present. His eye is upon the good and the evil. Develop a good relationship with God and you should have no trouble developing a decent one with others. Fellowship or communion is needed so don't sell yourself short with fly by night rendezvous. Take your time savor the moment and count the cost of waiting the best God has to offer. You will be glad you did. The Bible says, "They that wait upon the Lord shall renew their strength. They shall mount up with wings of an eagle. They shall walk and not be weary they shall run and not faint."

We made a church covenant to watch over our brothers and sisters in our fellowship, to walk circumspectly, to train our children in the way they ought to go. We will engage to seek the salvation of family and friends and to be our brother's keeper. We endeavor in our deportments to be fair in our dealings with others, aid each other in sickness and in distress, cultivate Christian sympathy and courtesy to all and seeking reconciliation we will strive for Christian love from station to station and as soon as we unite to carry out the same spirit and covenant of grace we agreed to on the principles of God's Word (Church Covenant, 2014).

We see three key concepts come out of this:

(1) Fellowship means now I am part of a body or group of people and I no longer have to be alone or isolated or in solitude. Fellowship gets rid of individualism or introverted state of mind I find myself in. Of course, it does not stop there because we can be in a crowd of people and even share certain things in common, but still not have fellowship (Keathley, 2004).
(2) Fellowship means we come together to share our interests, feelings, beliefs, what we do in the workforce, our hobbies, experiences, concerns, responsibilities, and purposes. Having or sharing

with others certain things gives us insight and understanding for the next level in our lives (Keathley, 2004).

(3) Fellowship can mean a *partnership* that involves working together and caring for one another as a company of soldiers or members of a military family. The FRG or Family Readiness Group can play an important role in this (Keathley, 2004).

Conclusion

Finally, let us be forgiving in our fellowship with one another, trust in Christ and His completed work, not judgmental or critical. In this fellowship we have to see ourselves as special and vitally important to the work of the ministry. For what pleases God is when we allow our fellowship and praise be unto the Lord in doing His will toward one another, especially helping and sharing His love with others (Abrams III, 2014).

"This is how I want you to conduct yourself in these matters. If you enter your place of worship and, about to make an offering, you suddenly remember a grudge a friend has against you, abandon your offering, leave immediately, go to this friend and make things right." Then and only then, come back and work things out with God.

"Or say you're out on the street and an old enemy accosts you. Don't lose a minute. Make the first move; make things right with him. After all, if you leave the first move to him, knowing his track record, you're likely to end up in court, maybe even jail. If that happens, you won't get out without a stiff fine. (Matthew 5:23-26, MSG)

When we have grievance against another or they have a grievance against us, we are unable to serve and help or encourage let alone be available. That is why the Bible says when at the altar to remember, "thy brother is against thee then go lay your gift at the altar and go be reconciled to thy brother then offer thy gift unto the Lord" (Matthew 5:24). Let us follow the process for making our love complete in Christ so we can share and have fellowship one with another according to Christ's standards. Good relationship with God brings good fellowship with others. Broken relations, where you can't hug your brother or sister, worship is broken. Set relationship back in order so fellowship can be restored.

References

Abrams, C.P. III. (2014). (2014).. What is True Biblical Fellowship? http://bible-truth.org/msg123.html

Bloom, J. (2013). Five Ways to Refresh the Saints in Your Life. http://www.desiringgod.org/blog/posts/five-ways-to-refresh-the-saints-in-your-life

DeYoung, K. (2012). Real Christianity. http://realchristianity.wordpress.com/2012/02/29/do-not-forsake-the-assembly-why-church-attendance-is-important/

Evans, D. (2012).What Christians Want to Know. http://www.whatchristianswanttoknow.com/bible-verses-about-fellowship-21-scripture-quotes/

Hunt, J. (2014). 52 Ideas for Fellowship in Your Small Group. Church leaders lead better every day. http://www.churchleaders.com/smallgroups/small-group-articles/152387-52-ideas-for-fellowship-in-your-small-group.html

Keathley, J.H. III. (2004). Christian Fellowship. bible.org. https://bible.org/article/christian-fellowship

Mahoney, K. (2014). Why Is Christian Fellowship So Important? http://christianteens.about.com/od/christianliving/a/Why-Is-Christian-Fellowship-So-Important.htm

Richards, L.O. (1990).The 365 Daily devotional commentary. USA. Victor Books

Minister Judy Wyndham
4456 Kobashigawa Street
Honolulu, Hawaii 96818

Biography

    Judy Wyndham was born and raised, born again and raised up in Chicago, Illinois. She confessed Christ as Lord and Savior at the early age of eleven and served God at the Jackson Boulevard Christian Church singing in the choir. From there, Judy became a member of the Lighthouse Baptist Church serving faithfully until God catapulted her to Apostolic Church of God baptizing her in the name of our Lord and Savior Jesus Christ and filling her with the precious Holy Ghost. Judy has also served faithfully at the Moody Church in Chicago as a Lay Counseling Minister and Information Specialist for the Church under the Pastoral guidance of Erwin and Rebecca Lutzer. Judy graduated from Trinity Evangelical Divinity School with a Masters Certificate in Biblical Studies and a four-year audit of the Masters of Divinity Degree. Judy has lived in Zion, Illinois and served on the Mothers Board four years at Christian Faith Fellowship Church in Zion, Illinois under Bishop James and Pastor Deborah Logan.

    Judy moved to Alpharetta Georgia in 2003 and served faithfully as Deaconess and Minister to Global Destiny Church under Bishop Thomas and Juanita Bynum Weeks III in Duluth Georgia. Judy has served faithfully in Dublin California for Camp Parks Chapel in the ministry of prayer and intercession and praise and worship under Chaplain Matthew Holder. Judy currently resides in Honolulu,

Hawaii with her family and has served faithfully in ministerial leadership at Center of Deliverance Church of God in Christ in Waipahu, Hawaii under Bishop Jesse T. and Lady Darlene Wilson as Minister of the Gospel, Praise and Worship Team Ministry, Shepherd Care Leader, Urban Initiatives Vice President for the Hawaii Jurisdiction. Judy Wyndham currently serves the Lord in ministerial leadership under Chaplain Anthony J. Cook at Tripler Army Medical Center Gospel Chapel.

Judy preaches the gospel of Jesus Christ when called upon and has served as Sunday School Superintendent and bible study teacher. Judy also shares her gift of intercession and prayer with the Tripler Chapel under the leadership of Chaplain Anthony J. Cook. By God's grace, Judy has acquired an Associate's Degree in General Studies, Bachelor's Degree in Criminal Justice, and a MBA in Marketing from Colorado Technical University. She is currently working on a Doctorate in Psychology from Grand Canyon University. She is an actively engaged prayer warrior and facilitates and oversees a prayer ministry called Midnight Oil of Prayer. She is blessed to have two sons, Derrick and daughter in love Vicky, and Al Pearson Jr., a daughter Chaundra Nicole, son-in-love Kenneth Gore, and twelve grandchildren. Judy is truly blessed and highly favored of the Lord and her purpose is to praise the Lord. You can contact Judy by email: prayerfirst@yahoo.com.

Shalom
Minister Judy Wyndham

www.ingramcontent.com/pod-product-compliance
Ingram Content Group UK Ltd.
Pitfield, Milton Keynes, MK11 3LW, UK
UKHW022218230426
12048UKWH00016BA/922